LLC

LLC Quick start guide – A beginner's guide to Limited liability companies, and starting a business

Table of Contents

Introduction 5
Chapter 1: Definition of an LLC 6
Chapter 2: Why you need an LLC 11
Chapter 3: LLC Rules and Regulations 13
Chapter 4: Creating an LLC 16
Chapter 5: How LLCs are taxed 24
Chapter 6: LLC Accounting 28
Chapter 7: LLC Member Rights 33
Chapter 8: LLC Limitations 36
Chapter 9: Dissolving an LLC 39
Conclusion 42

Copyright 2016 - All rights reserved.

The follow eBook is reproduced below with the goal of providing information that is as accurate and reliable as possible. Regardless, purchasing this eBook can be seen as consent to the fact that both the publisher and the author of this book are in no way experts on the topics discussed within and that any recommendations or suggestions that are made herein are for entertainment purposes only. Professionals should be consulted as needed prior to undertaking any of the action endorsed herein.

This declaration is deemed fair and valid by both the American Bar Association and the Committee of Publishers Association and is legally binding throughout the United States.

Furthermore, the transmission, duplication or reproduction of any of the following work including specific information will be considered an illegal act irrespective of if it is done electronically or in print. This extends to creating a secondary or tertiary copy of the work or a recorded copy and is only allowed with express written consent from the Publisher. All additional right reserved.

The information in the following pages is broadly considered to be a truthful and accurate account of facts and as such any inattention, use or misuse of the information in question by the reader will render any resulting actions solely under their purview. There are no scenarios in which the publisher or the original author of this work can be in any fashion deemed liable for any hardship or damages that may befall them after undertaking information described herein.

Additionally, the information in the following pages is intended only for informational purposes and should thus be thought of as universal. As befitting its nature, it is presented without assurance regarding its prolonged validity or interim quality. Trademarks that are mentioned are done without written consent and can in no way be considered an endorsement from the trademark holder.

Introduction

Thank you for taking the time to pick up this book about setting up an LLC.

This book covers the topic of LLCs (Limited liability companies) and will explain to you all about how they work and how to set one up!

Using an LLC as your business structure is an important part of protecting yourself and your assets from potential lawsuits. This liability protection that an LLC offers is a big attraction to business owners and people starting new businesses every day.

Having protection from lawsuits is one of the smartest things you can do for yourself and your business. In this book I'm going to take you step by step through the process of starting your LLC and I'll show you in detail the documents that you will need to make your LLC legal.

We will cover the Operations Agreement which is the document used as the foundation of your business. It contains the rules and regulations of your business in addition to outlining what the responsibilities and rights of the individual members are.

You will also learn how an LLC is taxed and what it means to have pass-through profits and losses. You will see many ways in which an LLC is a flexible entity. At the completion of this book you will have a good understanding of the LLC system, why you might want to establish one, and how to go about doing so.

Once again, thanks for taking the time to read this book, I hope you find it to be helpful!

Chapter 1:
Definition of an LLC

The letters LLC are the abbreviation for Limited Liability Company. Essentially this type of legal business arrangement separates the assets and liability of the owner of the company from that of the company itself. If a person owns an LLC that has debts, then the creditors can only go after the assets of the LLC and not the actual business owners themselves.

The people who own an LLC are referred to as members. These members are ruled by an operating agreement that they create when they first form the LLC. An LLC is formed legally by filing a documents called 'the articles of organization' with a state official, normally the Secretary of State. Every state has individual laws regarding what constitutes an LLC. However, in all states, all LLCs must be created by corporations or individuals legally capable of forming a business. There are businesses that are not allowed to be considered an LLC which include things like insurance companies and banks due to the nature of those businesses. Whenever you find yourself in the process of forming a new business, you are going to want to look into the local rules regarding LLCs just to ensure that you dot the I's and cross the T's.

An LLC is governed by a document that is written by the founding member(s) called the Operating Agreement. This document outlines all of the rules of the LLC. It also records the members' shares in the LLC and the amount of profits and losses that may be allocated to them. The Operating Agreement covers things such as voting, meetings, buying other members out, and dissolution LLC. It is one of the first documents written when the LLC if formed and it is the most important as it will allow you to set the rules of your LLC instead of having to follow the state rules.

One of the first decisions that you will have to make concerns how the new LLC will be structured. This is perhaps one of the most important decisions you will make for the company, bar none, and it should not be taken lightly as it is going to ultimately determine how much you will end up paying in taxes, the amount of paperwork you end up having to do, and the amount of personal liability you will have, which will also affect your ability to get loans for your business. How you end up forming your business will depend on the laws of the state where you have your business.

Below are some of the most common business structures. Once you understand them, you will be able to then decide for yourself how forming an LLC will compare with having either a corporation, a partnership, or a sole proprietorship. When choosing one of these business structures, you need to base your decision on the circumstances of you, the business owner. It will depend on your liability, the taxation you want, and the recordkeeping that you want to do.

Sole Proprietorship

This is the least complicated way that you can structure your business. It's very simple in that all of the control goes completely to the owner. As the name implies, a sole proprietorship is a company that is owned exclusively by a single person. However, as simple as that seems, it is good to keep in mind that this type of company does not protect the owner from any hardships or debts the business incurs. This means that if the business should be sued, the owner takes the full brunt of that as well, and their personal assets will be at risk.

A Sole Proprietorship can be any type of business as long as it is not a hobby or an investment. If you proceed down this route it is extremely important to consult an accountant to ensure you keep track of all the tax data you need to provide as a sole proprietorship.

Furthermore, you will want to keep in mind that sole proprietor companies do not have any business income that is automatically taxed, nor will they generate a typical tax form at the end of the year. Rather, you will incur a penalty if you do not make payments quarterly that cover taxes related to Medicare as well as social security. These payments will cover traditional income tax as well as the taxes you have to pay as a self-employed individual.

Partnership

If you will have one or more people along with you in your business venture, then you might form a Partnership. This means that everyone is contributing money, time, skills, and property to the business, and they all see equal returns. For partnerships you will not pay traditional income tax, and instead pay taxes on the return that the partnership generated in a given year.

When filing taxes, each partner will report their income on a 1040 tax form. You must report your income and pay your own taxes, as they will not be withheld automatically because partners and employees are two different things. This means that as a partner you must make quarterly self-employed tax payments in order to avoid fees. General full time partners are required to also pay the rate for self-employment when it comes to any net earnings generated by the partnership. Those who are considered limited partners are only going to be on the hook for paying a self-employment rate on payment generate from professional fees or services rendered.

Corporation

Corporate structures are a little more involved than other structures. They have more regulations and tax requirements that you have to comply with. So you may deal with more tax preparation services then you would with a sole proprietorship or a partnership.

Corporations do not function the way partnership's or sole proprietorships do, in this instance the individual person or individuals who own the business do not assume liability for the actions of the corporation. The corporation is held accountable as if it were its own person. It is also taxed the same way.

Income coming into the corporation is then taxed separately at corporate tax rates. A normal corporation is referred to as a C corporation. That's because details relating to it can be found in subchapter C of Chapter 1 of the IRS code. There is another corporation called a Subchapter S corporation. In this corporation you can pass income or losses through to the individual tax return of the owner of the business or the corporation. The rules are of course found in the first chapter of the IRS code in subchapter S.

S Corporations use a majority of the same types of corporate structures that a C Corporation does, but they are exempt when it comes to paying Federal taxes as well as passive income and capital gains. This type company pays taxes at the corporate level.

Limited Liability Company (LLC)

When it comes to business types, the LLC is actually relatively new on the scene. They are very popular because they are both cheap and easy to get, while also providing a wide-ranging list of protections that are in nearly every business owner's best interests. Additionally, some of the benefits of an LLC are similar to a partnership in that they allow for flexibility in management of the business, and they have the benefit of taxes being passed through.

The owner of an LLC type business is referred to as a member. Members can be anyone from individuals, to corporations, to other LLCs, as well as foreign entities. The majority of states also permit LLCs with only one owner, referred to as single LLCs. Banks and Insurance companies cannot be an LLC. Before forming an LLC, you should check your states guidelines to make sure that your type of business fits the requirements.

An LLC is ruled through its Operating Agreement which is written by its members. Although states do have different regulations regarding LLCs, there is still flexibility in the way that they can govern themselves. In this Agreement, the members have the opportunity to override the state rules and run their business somewhat by their own rules.

Chapter 2:
Why you need an LLC

One of the most basic reasons that people in business choose to form an LLC is to protect themselves in the event that they get sued. An LLC generally offers more protection than the other business structures. An LLC will insulate its members from the personal liability that can come with business matters. While individual LLC members are still accountable in the eyes of the law, when it comes to things like illegal activities, they won't be called to explain decisions made by representatives of the company. The same is true for all debts that the company owes - if it goes bankrupt those debts are not passed on to the owners.

Another plus to having an LLC is that you will avoid double taxation. The owners of profitable companies that are not corporations often have to take their profits in the form of dividends which are taxed more heavily than the type of profits that a corporation produces. An LLC is different in that it has the option to be considered what is known as a pass through entity. This means that it doesn't pay a type of income tax as an entity, and any losses or profits are then claimed by individual LLC members instead. Any earnings generated in this fashion are considered regular income and are then taxed appropriately.

If the LLC has members that are considered non-active, which means they own part of the company but do not actively work for it, then their earnings will be taxed via capital gain rates instead. If the LLC ends the year with a net loss instead of a net gain, then the LLC members will be able to use that loss as a way to minimize their personal tax liabilities for the year in question.

Another reason that an LLC is a great idea is that profit sharing is flexible. One of the biggest advantages you have with a pass-through entity is the way that business losses and personal income can be looked at subjectively in order to get the most out of the deal. But this will only work if you have income that is in need of being offset. If income and loss levels are lining up for some LLC members and not for others, then the amount that each member claims as a loss can easily be changed as long as the total amount works out to be the same.

You can solve this issue by changing the percentage of losses that each member of the LLC gets, in order to maximize their tax benefits. Members of LLCs are allowed to allocate their profits and losses however they want, whereas members of partnerships and S corporations aren't. An example being that two members of an LLC can split profits equally between themselves, but they can allocate more losses to one member.

Another great reason to form an LLC is that the organization of the company is much simpler. Simpler doesn't mean non-existent, however, and it is important to follow all of your state guidelines to ensure things are on the up and up. Nevertheless, you will spend much less time and money then you would if you were creating a corporation.

Chapter 3:
LLC Rules and Regulations

Each state has their own laws that govern LLCs. However, in most states, LLC members are allowed to conduct their businesses on their own or with partners. And unlike corporations, there aren't shareholder meeting or any annual meeting requirements when you form an LLC.

In every state there are certain documents that you need to have in order to create an LLC. The official documents will of course vary by state, but will include the Operating Agreement as well as the Articles of Organization. These articles will list the name of the LLC, the type of business, the names and addresses of the members managing the business, and the address of the business.

The Operating Agreement describes how the business will be run and will break down the rights of each of the LLC's partners. Depending on the state that you live in, one or both of these forms will be needed at the time that you file to form your LLC. You can find this information by contacting the Secretary of State, the State, or the Department of Commerce and Consumer Affairs.

You must file the Articles of Organization and/or Operating Agreement, as well as pay the required fee in your state in order to establish your LLC legally. Each state has a division that will accept corporate filings and provide you with the necessary copies and receipts.

The owner of an LLC is referred to as a Member. Single owner or single member LLCs are acceptable. An LLC can be run by members, managers or both. The difference between members and managers is that members are typically non-working owners, while managers are more hands on owners who will step in and oversee the daily operations of the business. An LLC has the option to decide how it will be managed. This is unlike a corporation, who automatically allows its shareholders, corporate officers, and board of directors to have a say in company decisions. The flexibility of an LLC is one of the biggest reasons that people are so drawn to using this business structure.

An LLC is not directly taxed by the IRS. Rather, LLCs with only one member are automatically considered sole proprietorships unless they file as a corporation when it comes to taxation. An LLC with anything greater than a single member is typically taxed in the same way a partnership is. In these cases, the profits and losses can be passed through to each partner to file on their own individual income tax return. These LLCs with more than one member can also choose to be considered as corporations for tax purposes.

Financial contributions are made to the LLC by the members bringing assets into the business and making an initial contribution. The general rule is that each member has an ownership interest equal to the percent of the amount they originally contribute. Then, if the company is ever sold or dissolved, this percentage that has been contributed will establish the portion of the assets that each member is entitled to receive. The one thing to keep in mind however is that no matter how much each member contributes, the owners are free to distribute ownership, interest, profits, and losses in whatever manner they choose.

There are exceptions to the LLCs Limited Liability. One of the major benefits of choosing an LLC is the Limited Liability that it gives. However, this does not make members invincible and if they abuse the rules they will be punished regardless. Here are a few examples:

- Treating the LLC funds as though they were personal funds

- Using the LLC as a cover for reckless, illegal, fraudulent or violent activities that directly cause harm to another individual

- Actively choosing to avoid paying federal or state taxes of any kind

- Withholding employee taxes and not transferring them to the proper authority

- Knowingly placing a personal guarantee on a business debt or other type of loan that you know the LLC will default on

Doing any of these things listed above will hold the member or members personally liable for whatever is going on. They will not be protected by the LLC liability.

Chapter 4:
Creating an LLC

Forming an LLC is simple. In this chapter we will look at just what you need to do. You must keep in mind that the documents that you need when you are registering your LLC will vary by state. We will however cover the main two documents required in most states.

First things first, your LLC is going to need a name and this name must follow all of the local rules regarding naming conventions. The rules will vary from state to state, but are usually a version of the following:

- There cannot be two LLCs with the same name on file

- You must use an LLC designator at the end of your business name such as "LLC", "L.L.C", "Ltd. Liability Co", "Limited Liability Company" or "Limited Company"

- You cannot use certain words such as Bank, Insurance, or Corporation. You should check with your state to see what other words are also prohibited.

You can call your state's LLC office and ask whether or not your chosen LLC name is available to you before you write it on your paperwork. There may even be the option for a fee to reserve the name until you can go in or mail in your paperwork.

Along with following your state's rules for naming, you will also need to take special care to avoid any trademark infringement. You can go to www.nolo.com/legalenclyopedia/business-name which is a list of every business currently active in the United States. Once you have found an available and legal name, you don't have to do anything right away. Instead, you will include the name in your Articles of Organization and it will be registered automatically as part of that process.

Articles of Organization

With a name in mind, you can pick up the Articles of Organization form at the State Filing Office. You will need to provide the name of your LLC, the address, and the names of the members (if required). Usually each one of the owners of the LLC would need to have a signature on the Articles of Organization, but a single member can be appointed to this task as well.

When you return the Articles of Organization to the state, you will also pay a filing fee. The fees are usually low. You end up paying around one hundred dollars. In some other states, California for example, you end up paying more. California charges an eight-hundred-dollar annual tax on top of the filing fee. In some states you will need to include the details of your LLCs registered statutory agent which is the person who is specifically designated to receive legal documents including court notifications.

The next step will be to create an operating agreement. Operating Agreements aren't always required to be filed in your states filing office at the time that you file the Articles of Organization. However, it is essential to create one. This is the document where you will set the rules for ownership as well as the details regarding the LLC's operations, similar to a corporation's bylaws. In some states, you will then be required to publish a notice in your local paper to make your company official.

This is a basic legal notice that indicates that the members of the LLC intend to form the organization in question. You will need to publish this notice in an officially licensed newspaper a certain number of times, depending on your state. You will then need to provide official verification that this has occurred, which is typically handled by the company you used to publish your notice in. Each state has different rules regarding this process and they can vary significantly.

After you have finished all of these steps, your LLC will be official. However, before you can actually start doing business, the LLC will need to procure the various permits and licenses that are required for business in your line of work, or any other permits/licenses required by your particular state or city.

Creating the Operating Agreement

I want to talk about the Operating Agreement here a little more in depth. The Operating Agreement is a very detailed document that is going to outline the rules and regulations on how you will run your business.

An Operating Agreement is also going to help you to safe guard your limited liability status. It will be key in the court respecting your LLC as a separate business entity when you have a written document. If you are a one member LLC, then this is very important for you since you don't want the court to see you as a sole proprietorship.

In the operating agreement it is important that you outline each member's share in the business, and also the business decision making rules. You also want to outline the way you will handle members leaving, and new members coming into the LLC. If you do not have these things outlined in your Operating Agreement, then it will be very hard to handle it if a member gets angry or upset at another member and complains. Also, if these things are not specified in the Operating Agreement, then if issues arise your business is at the mercy of the default state operating rules.

An example of overriding the states default operating rules would be the instance of investment. According to the state default rules, the LLC would be required to give out profits and losses equally among members. However, that would not be fair if each member contributed differently to the LLC. That is why in your Operating Agreement it is important to specify how each member contributes, and how the profits and losses are to be distributed among the members. By writing these things out in the Operating Agreement, you override the state's default operating rule.

There are many things that you are going to want to cover in your Operating Agreement. It is a very important document and you should take as much time as you need on it to ensure that nothing is missed. Every business is unique, and so is every Operating Agreement.

Here is a list of some of the general things included on most Operating Agreements:

- Members' responsibilities as well as rights
- What stake each member has in the company

- The voting power of the members'

- Allocation of profits and losses to each member

- Management of the LLC

- Meeting rules (how often, how long, etc.)

- Voting rules

- Details concerning the selling of shares once an owner wants to sell, passes away, or becomes unable to participate any longer.

Each of these items will require some decision making. If there are going to be several members or owners of your LLC, you will all want to get together and form this document together as it will affect all of you for the life of the LLC. Make sure that as you are drafting the document, you are specific and clear about the rules and what you are trying to say, so that there can be no misunderstanding if anyone goes to read it in the future.

Those who own an LLC normally will make contributions of services, property, time or other valuables in order to get the LLC on its feet, and are then rewarded with a share of ownership in the company proportionate to what they put in. However, one of the ways that having an LLC is flexible is that the members can decide to divide up ownership however they wish, no matter who has invested what to the LLC. It is very important that these contributions and ownership percentage decisions are recorded in your Operating Agreement to avoid arguments or disagreements in the future.

Not only do the LLC members receive a percentage of ownership in exchange for their investment, they also will receive distributive shares which are equal to the percent that they have invested in the LLC. These distributive shares are shares of the LLC's profits and losses.

Just like shares of ownership, most Operating Agreements will state that the shares of profits and losses are equal to the percentage that each member has contributed to the LLC. However, unlike with ownership of the LLC, the members can't just decide to change the percentages. They have to follow special allocation rules.

When you are drafting the financial part of your Operating Agreement, it may be a good idea to speak to a tax preparer regarding the allocation, just to make sure that what you are putting in your agreement is what you need to do to get the results that you want for your business.

Aside from the definition of each owner's share, your Operating Agreement needs to be able to tell you a few more things:

- How much of the LLCs profits will be allocated to the members each year.

- If the LLC will generate enough of a return for each member to cover taxes that will be paid in addition to the amount of the initial return. Members file taxes as being self-employed so they end up having to pay taxes to the state and the IRS based on the total amount of the profits as they are allocated on paper, regardless of what the reality of the matter turns out to be.

- If the LLC will make distributions regularly (ex. every two weeks) or can members make draws from the LLC as needed.

Since everyone has different financial situations and many fall into different tax brackets, how you distribute profits and losses is something that you must pay very close attention to. Again, make sure that it is all very clearly written in the Operating Agreement.

Most decisions within an LLC are made at informal meetings. However, there are times that there is a decision which is so big that something a bit more formal is required. In these cases, issues will be brought to a vote which can then be handled in two different ways.

- Each member's vote is equal to their amount of equity in the business

- Per Capita Voting – Meaning each member gets one vote

Your Operating Agreement should specify which voting method you are going to use should voting become necessary. No matter which method you choose, you need to make sure to specifically say how much voting power that each member has. You also need to specify how the vote will lead to a decision, specifically if any decision needs to be according to unanimous decision or majority rule.

An area where you may mention that you would need to take a vote would be in the event that there is dissolution of the LLC. If you have a multi member LLC it is a requirement that you take a vote to dissolve.

In your Operating Agreement, you will need to specify how your LLC will handle a buy-out of specific shares. You will want to cover such things as:

- Whether or not existing members can buy out the leaving members shares and keep control of the LLC

- Cost of purchasing the departing member's shares

- Are there other events that can cause a buy out and if so what are they? (could be an offer from an outside person to a member to buy their interest)

- Will you allow new members to join or only allow shares to be sold from existing member to member?

Not having a buyout agreement or these clauses in your Operating Agreement could cause the automatic dissolution of the LLC should a member leave. So it is very important to discuss these things with fellow members and make sure that they are included in your Operating Agreement.

Chapter 5:
How LLCs are taxed

Pass through LLC

Every LLC is automatically classified as a pass-through entity, as previously discussed. While this means that the LLC is not personally responsible for paying federal income taxes, those duties being passed on to their members, they may still be responsible for annual local taxes depending on what state it was created in. The number of individuals who own a portion of the LLC will determine if the IRS views the LLC as a partnership or a sole proprietorship instead.

When an LLC is considered a sole proprietorship, then all of the tax considerations are passed onto the proprietor, making it their responsibility to file federal returns each year as a schedule C entity and using a 1040 tax return. Additionally, you will then be required to pay income taxes related to any profit that was made as a result of the LLC. This remains the case even if you don't take the profits for personal use and instead leave them in the LLC's coffers for a rainy day. On the other hand, if multiple owners are involved, then the IRS will treat the LLC as a partnership which means that each partner will then be required to pay taxes on a portion of the overall total profits, based on the distribution that was decided when the LLC was created. They then still file a 1040 form before attaching a Schedule E document to cover the LLC partnership taxes.

When you form your LLC and fill out the Operating agreement, you decide what each member's percentage of income is in the LLC. If for some reason you decide to split the profits and losses in a percentage that is not the same as the percentages outlined in the operating agreement, then that would be called a special allocation. The IRS has special rules for this. The IRS pays very close attention to this so that they can be sure that there aren't any tax dollars being hidden by maybe giving all of the losses to the member in the highest income tax bracket. If for some reason the IRS rejects your special allocation request, you will then be taxed at the division of profits and losses outlined in your operating agreement.

It does not matter how the members decided to divide their shares of the company internally after the fact, the IRS will expect each member to pay their full share's worth of taxes each year unless shares are officially transferred beforehand. Additionally, a full tax payment will be required even if the member didn't take the full dispersal for use as personal funds as well. This remains true even if the funds are being used for business purposes or expansion as well. What's more, despite the fact that the LLC will not be liable for any income taxes itself, one of the members will still need to file what is known as a 1065 form come tax season. This form is then used by the IRS to ensure that individual members are being honest on their personal filing. This is in addition to a Schedule K-1 form that the LLC provides to each member detailing their profits (ideally) for the previous year. This form is filed in addition to the Schedule E, which is attached to the 1040 that each member will file with their individual return.

Corporate Taxation

If you find that you will be keeping a large amount of profits in your LLC bank account on a regular basis for expenses, you may want to consider choosing to have your corporation taxed as a corporate entity instead. This is as simple as filing form

8832 for the IRS, and electing the corporate tax classification option. This can be a good option because the tax rates for the first seventy-five thousand dollars are going to be lower when taxed at a corporate rate, because that is a small amount for a corporation to make, as opposed to the much higher rate that it would be charged for personal income if the members filed alone. This can easily save thousands per member, and is definitely worth looking into if you think your LLC might benefit from it. Choosing corporate taxation also gives the LLC a chance to offer members, as well as any LLC employees, a wide variety of other benefits as well, including tax advantages, stock options, and other fringe benefits.

Regardless, those who own part of an LLC are considered by the IRS to not be employed by a corporation, which makes them self-employed, and like all self-employed individuals they must pay their taxes quarterly to avoid paying fees. This means that each member will need to have an idea of what they are likely profit at the start of each year. This is so they can plan to make payments every four months. They must also make a payment to the state if there is a state tax. These payments are due in January, June, April, and September and will not include payments related to Medicare or Social Security, which will need to be made directly to the IRS as well.

The rule of thumb for this is the same as with the rest of the taxes, each member is responsible for the share of profits they receive or expect to receive as outlined in the Operating Agreement. However, inactive members who have invested money in the LLC but do not actively make decisions or provide any kind of work are not considered as being employed by the LLC, and are exempt from these rules.

Every member who is active and pays these taxes will report them on the Schedule SE which will need to be submitted annually. Additionally, be prepared to start paying about twice as much self-employment tax as the regular employees. This is largely due to the fact that as an employer you are going to be required to match employee contributions, though you will then at least be able to deduct half of the total from your taxes which may balance things out if you are lucky.

There are no taxes paid on most of the money that the LLC spends, and that includes business expenses which can be deducted before the total amount of income is determined. This is good because it can greatly reduce the profits you report to the IRS. For example; advertising costs, equipment costs, travel costs, and startup costs, among others. It is important to have a good and knowledgeable accountant to help you find all of the deductions that are allowable.

LLCs are taxed by the state in the same way that they are taxed by the IRS. As an LLC owner you will pay any LLC related tax penalties on your own tax returns. If the state you are living in charges the LLC a yearly tax, it will be based on the amount of income that the LLC brought in during the preceding 12 months. There are also states that charge LLCs an annual fee that has nothing to do with income - this is what is known as an annual registration fee, or possibly franchise tax, and typically is in the realm of $100. Before you form your LLC, you can find out about these extra taxes and fees that your state may charge you, and how much they will be so that you are not caught unaware come tax time.

Chapter 6:
LLC Accounting

Since most LLCs decide to be treated as a partnership for tax reasons, partnership accounting principles will apply. They are significantly different in the way that they operate than those used in a corporation. Let's go over some of the key terms.

Allocation and Distribution – Allocation refers to the actual dividing of the losses as well as the profits the LLC brings in among its members for tax and accounting purposes. This happens only on the books. Distribution is the actual transfer of the profits to the members. The timeframe for the distribution of profits and the allocation of profits and losses do not need to be the same however; for example, profits and losses are allocated once a year at tax time, while profits are distributed as a paycheck on a regular schedule.

Capital Accounts – Based on simple math, in this process each member is given a separate capital account which then includes a complete record of all of the profits and losses that member experiences in a given year. The money each member put in initially is then added to the amount of profit they earned in the given year, and that number is then used as the base from which to subtract any losses that they experienced in the same period, and the result is their tax penalty for the given period.

Profit and Loss Allocation – The allocation of losses as well as profits is initially determined based on what is outlined in the Operating Agreement. If an LLC should have a large early year loss, like in the case of a real estate holding company for example, members can then choose to allocate some of those losses based on the members with the largest capital accounts as it will do them the most good. This even includes passive members who will not be on the hook for as much, but may find a benefit in counterbalancing profits made elsewhere. Once the LLC begins earning profits again, the member accounts that were taken into the negative to balance out other gains will first be required to return to zero before any new profits can be generated.

Capital Transaction: Any transaction that can be considered an unusual way for the LLC to make a profit is considered a capital transaction. If a manufacturing company sold its factory, that would be an example of a capital transaction. On the other hand, any day-to-day transaction that generates a profit for the LLC through the everyday course of business is referred to as a non-capital transaction. You must treat these transactions differently because passive members of an LLC then have the chance to take losses from capital transactions only - they are not allowed to offset profits with non-capital transactions.

Compensating Managers and Members

There are two ways that Officers and or Shareholders in a Corporation can distribute the Corporations profits to themselves. First, they may write themselves a paycheck based on what their contributions have been to the Company.

And second, they may receive dividends on their stock. In this case, it doesn't matter what position you hold or how much work you do within the company. You are paid aggregate dividends based on how many shares you hold in the stock.

Remember we mentioned in the section about how an LLC is taxed that you can choose whether your LLC is treated as a corporation or as a partnership? Here we will discuss compensation as a partnership.

Salary vs. Draw – Corporations pay salaries to their employees regardless of whether or not those employees are shareholders. An LLC on the other hand, distributes draws against its year-end profits to its members. Unlike salaries, draws are in no way guaranteed. Corporations are committed to paying x amount of dollars per month in salaries. In an LLC, draws are only available as long as there are profits available. Members can agree to guarantee draws to one or more members. This does happen when there are members who are dependent on these draws or act as managers for the LLC.

Profit Distribution – In an LLC profits are distributed among members depending on their percentage of ownership in the business. Again they refer to the Operating Agreement to determine what percentage of the profits will go to each member. However, an LLC can be much more flexible than a corporation in the distributing of profits. In a corporation for example, they would offer different runs of stock or separate it into various classes if they hoped to offer different amounts to different members. Not so for LLC members who are always able to forego the Operating Agreement and distribute their profits any way that they see fit among themselves. For example, if there is a cash investor, they may decide to have that member receive a larger portion of the profits until their investment has been returned. An LLC is also unique in that it can customize its terms for a specific situation, and then change them back just as quickly, which alone gives the LLC many benefits over corporations.

Bookkeeping

Even though an LLC does not pay taxes itself, there are still some records that must be kept for tax purposes and in order to pay its members. The LLC must make sure that

The profit that comes in matches the amounts paid to the members. Here we will discuss some basic guidelines for keeping track of the LLCs expenses and profits.

Chart of Accounts – When you start your business you will most likely invest in some type of accounting software. Included in that software there will be a section called chart of accounts. You can enter all of your accounts and track them there. Under asset accounts, you can list your cash, receivables, and inventory, etc. Liability accounts would include your wages that you pay, loans, interest paid, etc. Owner's equity accounts will show how much the owners have invested into the company. Revenue accounts will show all of your profits received. Operating Expenses will include your rent, advertising, utilities, supplies, etc. Then you should also have a section to list profit earned for the sale of assets or interest.

Daily Entries – You should be making entries into your chart of accounts every day. Keeping this up to date is very important. You need to keep track of the checks you are writing and receiving, any money withdrawn by members, receipts for purchases made for the business, etc. The software will automatically add and subtract everything for you and you can produce reports for any of the accounts to see exactly where they stand. Accurate entries are crucial.

Pass-Through payments to Members – This is the one accounting practice that is unique to LLCs. An LLC must show how much money it is passing through to its members so that the IRS can collect tax payments from those members on their earnings from the LLC.

Tax Credits – There is no accounting to be done for tax credits for an LLC since an LLC does not directly pay taxes. All expenses are reported on a Schedule C.

Chapter 7:
LLC Member Rights

The rights of members in an LLC are controlled by the individual state statutes and by the individual LLC Operating Agreements. Forming an LLC has many advantages since it gives you a lot of flexibility in drafting your own unique rights and obligations in your Operating Agreement. Many people are drawn to this ability to modify their ownership and financial structure so that it's most effective for them.

In this chapter we will go over the basic rights of LLC members. Please keep in mind that they do vary by state so you again will have to check with your state for anything specific that you may want to include in your Operating Agreement.

Information and Records – As a member of an LLC, you have the right to see records and stay up to date on any financial statements, or any other significant records within the LLC. It is important for members to exercise their rights to see records and check the LLC from time to time to stay informed of their rights and of the LLC itself.

Right of withdraw - In your Operating Agreement, it should discuss the right of members to withdraw from the LLC prior to its closing. Typically, the way a member can withdraw is with the written consent of all other members. However, you can specify in your Operating Agreement a variety of ways that you can allow a member to withdraw from the LLC. You can specify certain events that may trigger member's rights to withdraw. Or you may restrict member's rights to withdraw like a statute. It's important for all members to understand the Operating Agreement and what their withdrawal rights are, so that they may develop an effective exit strategy if need be.

Right of Refusal – In some Operating Agreements there is given the right to purchase a withdrawing member's part in the LLC. Should a member decide to leave and sell his/her share to someone else, then the right of refusal is triggered. One of the benefits to this right is the ability to keep control of the LLC. Including this right when you create your Operating Agreement can eliminate potential issues down the road if a member decides to withdraw, because you won't have a new person then coming into the LLC to take their place. You can simply have a current member take over the withdrawing members share.

Distributions – LLCs are not required to make distributions to members. If an LLC is not able to pay its bills, and it runs the risk of going broke, then it cannot pay distributions. In the state of Washington, once a member gets to the point that they are able to earn distributions; their status becomes a creditor to the LLC. Again, the way that you will allocate distributions in your LLC will be outlined in your Operating Agreement.

Independent Counsel – Every member of an LLC has the right to his or her own independent counsel. In order to make sure that you are protected as a member, it is a good idea to sit with a business attorney and review the Operating Agreement as well as any other founding documents provided to you by the LLC. Even if you see that the Operating Agreement has been drafted by an Attorney, it is still always a good idea for a second pair of eyes to look it over.

The flexible nature of the LLC has made it very popular for business owners and entrepreneurs. However, because of its flexibility, it also allows for Operating Agreements to be drafted with many more restrictions, or not enough restrictions for LLC members. That's why before you enter into any agreement you should make sure that you read, understand, and most importantly agree with all of the rights and obligations outlined in the Operating Agreement before becoming part of the LLC.

Chapter 8: LLC Limitations

While an LLC structure certainly has many advantages and offers many freedoms in the choices you can make, it does have its share of limitations. In this chapter we will look at what those limitations are.

There are several states that still will require that an LLC be made up of more than one member. So if you live in a state where that is a case, you can look at using a carefully drafted grantor trust to serve as the second member. This does serve as a benefit to you as it also reinforces the limited liability aspect of the LLC. The income would still be reported on the members' 1040 tax return.

Limited Liability Companies are not always available in states for those with a professional practice such as doctors and lawyers. If you have a professional practice, you should always check with your state to see what their rules are before attempting to form an LLC for yourself.

There are limitations to the liability in an LLC. Hence, it is called limited liability. There are three different situations in which a member of an LLC can be held liable for different claims.

- If a member commits an act of omission or negligence, fraud, or some other illegal act.

- If a member personally guarantees a contract that they shouldn't

- If a member consents to receive or distribute funds in violation of the LLCs operating agreement

These claims are not limited to only an LLC, but can be applied to a corporation as well.

In order for you to protect yourself using the liability protection that the LLC offers, you must follow the rules for running the LLC very strictly. Make sure that the LLC has its own bank account and make sure that you are treating it completely as a business. Otherwise, should you be sued, there is still that chance that someone may be able to get to your personal assets.

When you have an LLC as your business structure it does not mean that you will have better access to loans. In fact, you will probably still have to sign a personal guarantee to take out loans for your LLC. That is at least until you have established a good relationship with a lender. Unfortunately, this also means that should the LLC default on the loan, you will be personally responsible to pay the loan.

Investors and sources of capital are a little harder to find if you have an LLC. They are hesitant because of the larger legal obligations and the more detailed state filings involved when adding new members to an LLC, which they would have to become in order to invest. So if you are running a company that is internet based and needs venture capital to grow quickly, this could be a limitation that could be a large disadvantage. In this situation, it would be wise to have investors and capital lined up at the creation of your LLC.

If you plan to expand your business and grow into other states, the fact that each state can have different rules to govern LLCs can be a dilemma. Depending on how many states you decide that you would like to do business in, it may become difficult to keep track of and abide by all of the different requirements that each state has. It may then be easier just to form subsidiary entities to operate in those other states.

Chapter 9:
Dissolving an LLC

If at some point down the road, you and/or your partners decide to dissolve your LLC for any reason, there will be certain legal steps that you need to take. Here we will take a look at dissolving an LLC with more than one member. Then we will go through dissolving a one member LLC, or sole proprietorship.

The first thing that will happen is that you and your fellow members will need to cast a vote with the goal of disbanding the LLC. If your LLC has more than just members and also includes a board then the board will need to vote on the dissolution as well.

Next, you will have to write the Articles of Dissolution for the LLC. This will be necessary in order to separate yourself and each member of the LLC from the LLC. You will then file this paperwork with your state agency. At the time that this paperwork is filed, all of the LLCs taxes must be paid and all debts must be current.

The next step is to cancel all of the LLC licenses and permits, which will need to be done on a one-by-one basis. If you are dissolving your LLC and entering into another business, some of these licenses and permits may actually be transferrable and that may be something that you will want to ask your state agencies about.

You will have to cancel your Employee Identification number and unregister your business name, which will typically include notifying the IRS of what you are doing as well. When you cancel your employee identification number this will alert the IRS that you have dissolved the LLC and they will refer to it as account closure. You will also have to contact your state agency to withdraw your business name.

As you are doing these things, you want to keep track of receivables coming in, and make sure that you are getting all monies owed to you on any accounts you have open. You will also need to give notice to your creditors and clients. A good way to do this would be to mail notices to everyone, and let them know of your intentions to close your business and that you will be paying off any balances you owe whether it is through the LLC, a settlement, or through bankruptcy, depending on the reason for dissolving your LLC.

After you have paid remaining debts, the last thing that you must do is distribute the remaining assets of the LLC among its members. You will follow the rules in your Operating Agreement as well as your states laws regarding distribution of assets.

Sole Proprietorship

In a single member LLC, the dissolution is very similar, with a few exceptions. Obviously you don't have to vote to dissolve. And you don't have to follow any rules to distribute the assets of the LLC. Everything else however, is basically the same. You still will have to file the required paperwork and cancel licenses and permits. If your licenses and permits are close to renewal, you can simply let them expire. That saves the step of going to the issuing authority to have them canceled. You still must pay taxes and outstanding debts, and make sure that you owe zero outstanding balances. You can file a Schedule SE with your income tax paperwork and send that to the IRS. There is no need to send any other type of paperwork to them.

Then, you may sell any equipment that you do not wish to keep.

Conclusion

Thanks again for taking the time to read this book!

You should now have a good understanding of how an LLC works, and how to create one!

If you enjoyed this book, please take the time to leave me a review on Amazon. I appreciate your honest feedback, and it really helps me to continue producing high quality books.

www.ingramcontent.com/pod-product-compliance
Lightning Source LLC
LaVergne TN
LVHW020447080526
838202LV00055B/5367